Dung Beetles

Clint Twist

GARETH**STEVENS**

GS PUBLISHING

A Member of the WRC Media Family of Companies

Please visit our web site at: www.garethstevens.com
For a free color catalog describing Gareth Stevens Publishing's list
of high-quality books and multimedia programs,
call 1-800-542-2595 (USA) or 1-800-387-3178 (Canada).
Gareth Stevens Publishing's fax: (414) 332-3567.

Library of Congress Cataloging-in-Publication Data

Twist, Clint.
    Dung beetles / Clint Twist. — North American ed.
      p. cm. — (Nature's minibeasts)
    Includes index.
    ISBN 0-8368-6374-7 (lib. bdg.)
    1. Dung beetles—Juvenile literature. I. Title.
  QL596.S3T93   2006
  595.76'49—dc22   2005044712

This North American edition first published in 2006 by
Gareth Stevens Publishing
A Member of the WRC Media Family of Companies
330 West Olive Street, Suite 100
Milwaukee, WI 53212 USA

This edition copyright © 2006 by Gareth Stevens, Inc. Original edition copyright © 2006
by ticktock Entertainment Ltd. First published in Great Britain in 2006 by ticktock Media Ltd.,
Unit 2, Orchard Business Centre, North Farm Road, Tunbridge Wells, Kent TN2 3XF.

Gareth Stevens series editor: Gini Holland
Gareth Stevens graphic designer: Dave Kowalski
Gareth Stevens art direction: Tammy West

Photo credits: (t=top, b=bottom, l=left, c=center) CORBIS: 22, 31t, 23t. FLPA Images: 2-3, 4t, 11bl, 12-13 all,
14-15 all, 17 all, 20, 21t, 29b. Image Bank: 16-17 main. PhotoDisk: 18-19 main, 20-21c.

Every effort has been made to trace the copyright holders for the photos in this book. The publisher apologizes
in advance for any unintentional omissions and would be pleased to insert appropriate acknowledgements in
any subsequent edition of this publication.

Printed in the United States of America

1 2 3 4 5 6 7 8 9 10 09 08 07 06

Words that appear in the glossary are printed
in **boldface** type the first time they occur in text.

CONTENTS

What Are Dung Beetles?

Dung beetles are medium-sized winged **insects**. They can be seen rolling balls of dung, or animal waste, along the ground. They often fall over, so they are sometimes called tumblebugs.

How do dung beetles live?

A dung beetle digs an underground burrow to live in. Males and females usually live in separate burrows. In some species, the males look different from the females. These males have horns on their heads.

What do they eat?

Dung beetles eat dung. Most of their dung comes from large, plant-eating **mammals** that graze on grass or eat the leaves of trees and shrubs.

A dung beetle feasts on cow **manure**.

UNDERSTANDING MINIBEASTS

Insects belong to a group of **minibeasts** known as **arthropods**. Adult arthropods have jointed legs but do not have inner **skeletons** made of bones. Instead, they have tough outer "skins" called **exoskeletons** that support and protect their bodies. All insects have six legs when they are adults. Most insects also have at least one pair of wings. Some have two pairs.

A giant dung beetle rolls a ball of dung.

Where do they live?
Dung beetles live anywhere that cattle, buffalo, horses, antelope, and other large mammals are found.

Brightly colored male and female dung beetles meet head to head.

All beetles belong to a group of minibeasts called arthropods.

5

A Dung Beetle Up Close

A dung beetle is often between 2 and 3 inches (40 and 70 millimeters) long. It has six legs and one pair of flying wings. Its body has three parts, the head, **thorax**, and **abdomen**.

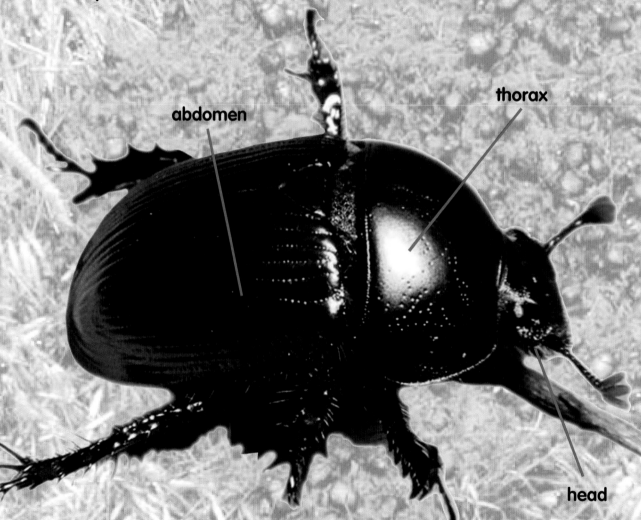

abdomen

thorax

head

The abdomen is the largest part of a dung beetle's body. It contains the **digestive system** and other important **organs.**

Beetles have only one pair of flying wings, the back pair. Instead of front wings, they have a pair of stiff, hard wing cases that are called **elytra**.

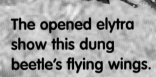

The opened elytra show this dung beetle's flying wings.

When the beetle is on the ground, the elytra fold over the flying wings. When the beetle is flying, the tough, unfolded elytra stick out to give the beetle more lift.

The head carries the **antennae**, eyes, brain, and mouth. The legs and wings are attached to the middle part of the body, the thorax.

SIX LEGS

Beetles and other insects are sometimes called hexapods because they all have six legs. *Hex* means six in Latin. All insects are hexapods, but not all hexapods are insects.

Like all other hexapods, dung beetles have six legs.

A World of Dung

Dung is the solid waste material produced by plant-eating mammals. Plants have less energy in them than meat. Plant eaters have to eat larger amounts of food than meat eaters, which means plant eaters make large amounts of solid waste.

For dung beetles, and many other minibeasts, the dung of plant-eating mammals provides a good supply of food.

No animal 's digestive system can digest all that the animal eats. Dung always contains partly-digested plant material, along with dead **bacteria** and useful **minerals.**

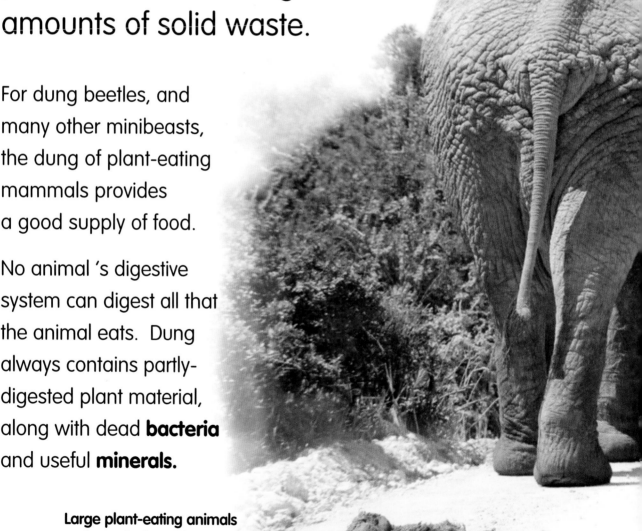

Large plant-eating animals such as elephants leave large piles of dung!

Dung beetles and other insects are part of nature's large, but mostly unseen, clean-up crew. Without these millions of minibeasts, the world's grasslands would become covered with a layer of dung. Some members of the clean-up crew get rid of dead bodies. Sexton beetles, for example, bury the bodies of small mammals and birds so their young can feed on the **corpses**.

This magnified view shows bacteria inside a dung pile.

When dung is left on the ground, bacteria from the air and the soil start to eat the dead bacteria and minerals in dung.

Fungi that grow in dung help break down the dung, which helps make the soil rich.

Some tiny plants and **fungi** grow only in dung. They are the dung beetle's main source of food.

Sexton beetles are often called burying beetles because they bury the corpses of small animals.

9

Something Smells Good

The smell of dung attracts dung beetles. More dung beetles are found where plant-eating animals live in great numbers because more dung is available in these areas.

When huge herds of mammals pass through grassland, such as the Serengeti Plain in Africa, they drop a lot of dung. On this plain, beetles looking for a meal can find it quickly.

Wildebeests graze on the plains of the Serengeti in Africa.

In **scrubland**, mammals are few and far between, and their dung is very scarce. New droppings attract hungry dung beetles from up to 900 yards (825 meters) away.

Beetles do not have noses. Instead, they use their antennae to smell the air. A dung beetle's antennae can pick up the slightest smell of dung.

antenna

BEST WAY TO TRAVEL?

Beetles, like most animals, normally travel headfirst. Their eyes and sense organs are located on the front of their heads, so they can check the world as they move forward. As we shall see with the dung beetle, however, headfirst is not always the best way to travel.

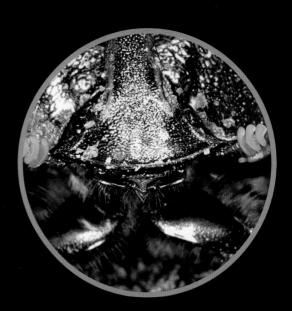

The head of a South American dung beetle is scoop-shaped.

Dung Mining

Minibeasts attack a pile of dung in many ways.
Some tunnel straight in to find the best bits.
Others are content to nibble at the edges.
Dung beetles usually are not too fussy
about the quality of the dung.

Dung beetles are well designed
and equipped as dung miners.
A strong, curved shield
protects the front of
the head.

**The edge of the beetle's head shield has notches
that look like the teeth on a steam shovel.**

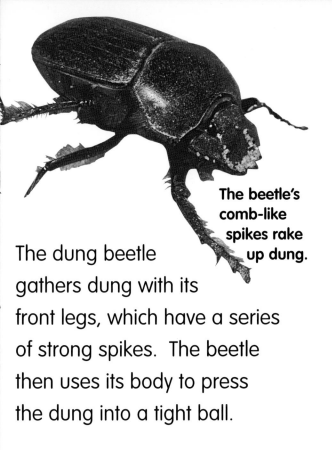

The beetle's comb-like spikes rake up dung.

The dung beetle gathers dung with its front legs, which have a series of strong spikes. The beetle then uses its body to press the dung into a tight ball.

The dung beetle uses its own weight to shape the dung into a compact ball.

HARD WORKERS

No matter how hard they work, dung beetles can never match the achievements of termites, which are the mining, construction, and engineering champions of the insect world. Termites build mounds of earth more than 13 feet (4 meters) high, with tunnels that reach about the same distance underground. It takes a team of millions of termites to build a mound. One termite by itself can do very little, but each dung beetle's ball is its own small achievement.

A termite mound towers above the grass in Africa.

Shaping the Ball

As a dung beetle collects more and more dung with its front legs, the compressed ball beneath its body gets bigger, like a snowball being rolled in the snow. Eventually, the ball gets so big that the beetle is tilted forward.

The dung beetle uses its powerful back legs to grip the ball and stay steady during the rolling process.

In this unusual position, the dung beetle uses its middle legs and back legs to make the ball even bigger.

These legs have tiny hooks on the ends that allow the beetle to get a good grip on its ball of dung.

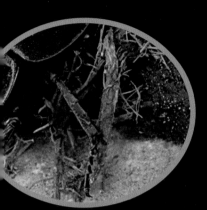

The hooks on the ends of dung beetles' legs are sharp.

The beetle can then turn the dung ball this way and that, to press every part of the ball's surface between its body and the ground with the same amount of pressure.

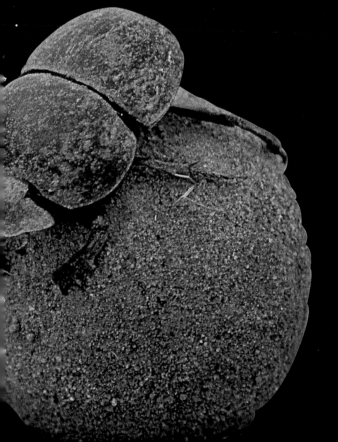

INSECT ENGINEERING

When human engineers want to measure the size, shape, and smoothness of a ball, they use an instrument called a pair of **calipers,** which has two pieces of curved metal joined together at one end. The middle and back legs of a dung beetle act like two natural calipers that help the beetle make perfectly shaped dung balls of exactly the right size.

The dung beetle's legs are so well placed on its body that it can roll perfect balls every time.

Rolling Home

When it is satisfied with the size and shape of its dung ball, the beetle starts pushing the ball back to its burrow. The beetle walks in a straight line, paying no attention to the slopes and curves of the ground.

The dung beetle walks backward to make its return trip. Its front legs are useless for controlling the ball. It takes all four middle and back legs to steer the ball in a straight line.

Walking backward in a straight line over bumpy ground is very difficult, even without pushing a huge ball of dung!

A pair of European dung beetles struggle to push a ball up a steep sand bank.

The flower beetle is a shiny green dung beetle.

Nearly every journey has its mishaps and setbacks. The dung beetle's frequent falls have given it the nickname "tumblebug."

MUSCLE POWER

Although the dung beetle might seem to make very slow and uneven progress, it is usually successful. It succeeds because of its insect muscle power. A beetle pushing a dung ball across 328 feet (100 m) of grassland is equal to one person pushing a small car about 2 miles (3 kilometers) over rough ground that is covered with thick jungle.

Pushing a dung ball over rough or grassy ground is hard work for a dung beetle.

Underground Pantry

Sometimes, the tasty dung ball is eaten as soon as the beetle gets back to its burrow. Often, however, the dung ball is stored in the burrow to provide food for times when fresh dung is scarce.

In many places, dung is scarce all year round. Even on the best grasslands, it can become scarce at times. When, for example, the herds of mammals on the Serengeti leave for fresh pastures, the amount of dung available for dung beetles drops dramatically.

Wildebeests prepare to migrate from the Serengeti Plain in Africa.

Although the outside of the ball might dry out, the dung in the middle of the ball will stay moist, and the

The inside of a dung ball stays damp.

tasty plants and tiny fungi inside the ball will continue to grow. Fortunately, a well-rolled dung ball will stay good enough to eat for several months.

CRADLE OF DUNG

After mating, a female dung beetle carefully makes a special egg ball, choosing only the very best dung. She takes extra care on the homeward trip to make sure the surface of this ball is completely smooth. Inside the burrow, she lays her eggs in the middle of the ball, leaving just a single air hole so the eggs can breathe.

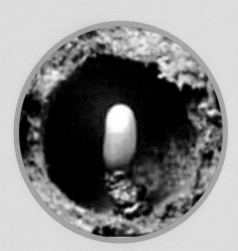

A single dung beetle egg rests inside a dung ball.

A Caring Mother

Among many dung beetle species, the females stay in the burrow with their eggs and guard them against **predators** and **parasites**. In the world of minibeasts, many species feed on the eggs of other species, just as, among larger animals, many creatures feed on birds' eggs.

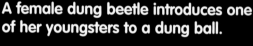

A female dung beetle introduces one of her youngsters to a dung ball.

This larva of a dung beetle is developing into a **pupa**.

If the female is successful, her eggs will soon hatch and **larvae** will come out. The larvae begin to feed on the tiny plants and fungi inside their dung ball.

They remain inside their cradle of dung until after they **pupate** and grow into their adult form.

The pupa of a dung beetle is tiny.

When the small beetles have eaten their way out of the dung ball, their mother walks them out of the burrow and introduces them to the wonderful world of dung.

INSECT DEVELOPMENT

Insects develop from eggs in two different ways. With many kinds of insects, including dung beetles, the eggs hatch into worm-like larvae. The larvae go through a stage called pupation, during which they change into adults. With many other kinds of insects, such as cockroaches and grasshoppers, the eggs hatch into **nymphs** that already have the body shape of an adult.

The larva of a dung beetle rests in a pupation cell or finds a safe place to stay while its body changes into a pupa.

Dung Beetles and Humans

The ancient Egyptians believed the dung beetle was a sacred insect. They called it a **scarab**, and that name is still used today. The scientific name for dung beetles is *Scarabaeidae,* so they are often referred to as scarab beetles.

The ancient Egyptians saw young beetles coming out of balls of dung and thought that they were a miraculous creation of life. They also thought that a scarab pushing its ball across the ground was like the Egyptian gods pushing the Sun across the sky.

This piece of Egyptian jewelry from the second century B.C. has a scarab in its center.

Many people wear good luck charms in the shape of scarabs. Charms are made of wood, stone, pottery, or glass.

THE SUCCESS OF FAILURE

In many ways, dung beetles are most useful when their colony dies, or when their stored food remains uneaten, or when their eggs fail to hatch. Their millions of uneaten dung balls provide a good way to mix dung into the soil. Dung, or, as farmers call it, manure, is a good fertilizer for land. When dung beetles fail in their own lives, their dung balls succeed in helping plants to grow.

In some parts of the world, people protect dung beetles. This sign in KwaZulu, Natal, South Africa, warns people to watch out for dung beetles that cross the road.

Unused dung balls help fertilize the soil when they rot.

Dung Beetle Variations

Thousands of species of dung beetles thrive in different parts of the world. They all have the same basic shape and follow the same basic patterns of behavior, but the details of their bodies and lives vary widely.

Shiny Scarab

Most dung beetles look dull, but some from tropical regions are very eye-catching. On this beetle (*right*) from South America, called a precious metal scarab, the elytra and the top of the head are a shiny, gold or silver color.

Most dung beetles collect their dung from big piles left by large mammals and have to work hard cutting and shaping each dung ball. Other dung beetles, such as the European minotaur beetle, have an easier job. They collect the dung of rabbits, which is exactly the right size and shape for these beetles and is ready to roll.

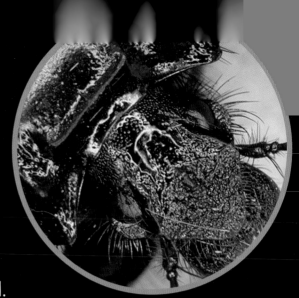

Too Big to Bury

In India, there is a species of dung beetle that rolls a dung ball much larger than normal, the size of an apple or an orange. This ball is much too big for the insect to bury. Instead, the beetle carefully coats the ball with a thick layer of mud. After the mud dries, it keeps the dung inside fresh.

No Rolling

Not every species of dung beetle collects dung balls. Aphodian dung beetles, which are only about .2 inches (5 mm) long when fully grown, tunnel into the soil beneath the right kinds of dung. After digging the burrows, aphodian dung beetles can then feed whenever they want, completely safe from predators such as birds.

Other Beetles

Species of beetles are found on Earth in greater numbers than any other kinds of insects. Scientists already know of about 400,000 beetle species, and new kinds of beetles are found almost every day.

Fireflies

Despite the name, fireflies are actually beetles. They are also called lightning bugs. Fireflies are found in woodland and grassland regions throughout the world. These beetles have special organs on their abdomens that produce flashes of green light. Each species has its own pattern of flashes. The fireflies use these patterns of flashing light to attract mates.

Weevils

Weevils are also known as snout beetles because they have narrow heads that end in a long snouts. The **jaws** are placed at the end of the snout. Most weevils are plant eaters and some species, such as the cotton-boll weevil, are terrible farm pests.

Diving Beetles

Diving beetles are some of the fiercest predators found in ponds and streams. The great diving beetles (*right*) are about 2 inches (50 mm) long and catch fish of even greater size in their powerful jaws. When they dive under water, they trap air beneath their wings and between the hairs on their abdomens.

Ladybugs

These dome-shaped beetles are easy to recognize by their patterns of spots. Some species, such as the seven-spot ladybug, always have the same number of spots. Others, such as the convergent ladybug, can have any number between two and thirteen. Ladybugs are well-liked by gardeners because they eat insect pests.

Life Cycle

Most dung beetle species reproduce in spring, summer, and fall, when the weather is warm. In some species, the female and male work together to dig a burrow and bring dung into it. In others, these jobs are done only by the female. In the burrow, the female dung beetle lays eggs that will hatch into larvae. The larvae develop into pupae. As the pupae feed on dung brought into the burrow, they grow into adult beetles and then dig their way to the surface. Most dung beetles live from three to five years.

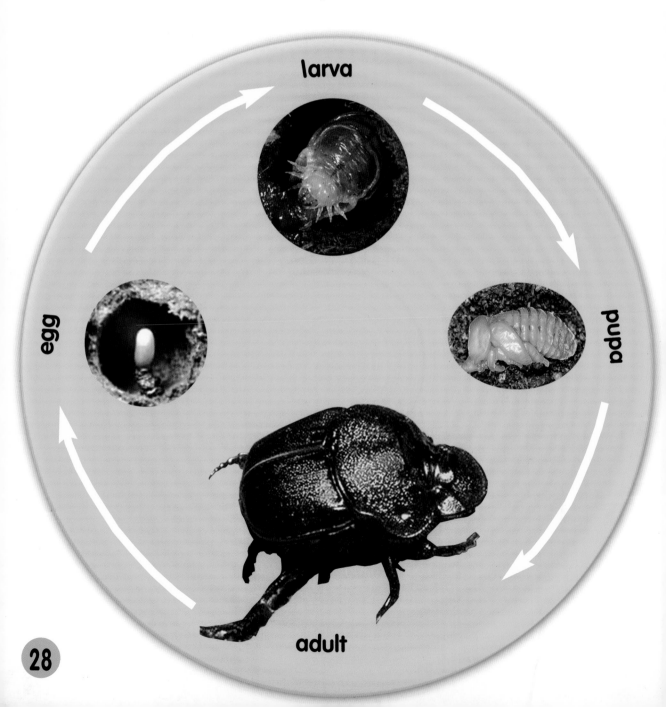

larva

egg

pupa

adult

Fabulous Facts

Fact 1: Dung beetles are a fairly new group of beetles. The oldest dung beetle fossils date back only forty million years, which is not a long time for insects.

Fact 2: Scientists have found six thousand species of dung beetles. Some of them only eat the dung of one certain animal, and no other.

Fact 3: Some tribes from South America believe a dung beetle named Aksak modeled the first man and woman out of clay.

Fact 4: In 1973, an incredible sixteen thousand dung beetles climbed onto a 3-pound (1.5-kilogram) pile of elephant dung on the African savannah in just two hours.

Fact 5: Some farmers brought dung beetles to Australia to stop flies from reproducing in cow dung. By eating the cow dung, these beetles got rid of a lot of the fresh dung that the flies needed to reproduce.

Fact 6: A dung beetle can bury two hundred and fifty times its own weight in a single night.

Fact 7: New research suggests that some dung beetles use moonlight at night to roll dung balls to safe spots.

Fact 8: One species of dung beetles spends most of its time living on a sloth, which is a mammal that lives in trees. When the sloth's droppings fall, the beetles drop onto the dung.

Fact 9: Scientists have found one kind of dung beetle that feeds only on human waste.

Fact 10: Dung beetles range from less than .039 inches (1 mm) in size to a giant 2.5 inches (6 centimeters).

Fact 11: A certain kind of dung beetle in South America feeds on the leavings of large snails. It rides around on their backs waiting for the waste to drop!

Fact 12: Some dung beetles eat and lay their eggs on dung that other beetles collect. Besides stealing the dung, they also eat the dung owners' eggs.

Fact 13: Dung beetles live on every continent except Antarctica, which is too cold.

Glossary

abdomen — the largest part of an insect's three-part body, containing most of its important organs

antenna/antennae — a pair of sense organs found at the front of the head on most insects. One-half of that pair is called an antenna.

arthropods — minibeasts, including insects and spiders, that have jointed legs

bacteria — microscopically small organisms that can live just about anywhere. Some bacteria can cause diseases.

beetles — one of a large group of insects that have wing cases, or elytra, to protect their flying wings

calipers — an instrument used by engineers to measure the diameters of circular shapes

corpses — the bodies of dead animals

digestive system — the organs in the bodies of animals that are used to process food

dung — the solid waste material made by animals' digestive systems

elytra — the stiff, hard wing cases that protect the flying wings of beetles

exoskeletons — hard outer coverings that protect and support the bodies of some minibeasts

fungus/fungi — a group of living things that are separate from plants and animals, including microscopic yeasts, large toadstools, and mushrooms. More than one fungus is called fungi.

insects — a kind of minibeast that has six legs; a body with three parts; and, in most cases, one or more pairs of wings

jaws — strong, hinged mouth structures that allow many animals to bite and chew

larva/larvae — the worm-like form of an insect after it hatches from an egg. More than one larva are called larvae.

mammals — warm-blooded animals that have an internal skeleton and feed their young milk from the mother's body

manure — the term for animal waste that farmers and gardeners often add to the soil to feed their plants

minerals — natural substances that are found in rocks and soil

minibeasts — all small land animals that do not have a skeleton inside their bodies

nymphs — the young of insects that do not produce larvae

organs — the parts of an animal's body that perform a certain task, such as the stomach, which digests food

parasites — living things that live in, on, or feed on the bodies of other living things without giving anything useful back to their hosts

predators — animals that hunt and eat other animals

pupa/pupae — the stage of certain insects' life cycles, during which a larva changes into the adult. More than one pupa are called pupae.

pupate — to change from a larva into an adult insect

scarab — the ancient Egyptian name for a dung beetle, the name sometimes used today to refer to any dung beetle

scrubland — land dotted with shrubs, grass, and small trees

skeletons — the inner structures of bones that support the bodies of animals such as birds, mammals, fish, and reptiles

thorax — the middle part of an insect's body, where its legs are attached

Index